LIVEaLIFE

SPREADING THE FRUITS OF THE

Love, Joy, Peace, Patience, Kindness, Goodness, Faithfulness, Gentleness, and Self-Control

BRENDA D. KEENE ("BEMMER")

WestBow Press books may be ordered through booksellers or by contacting:

WestBow Press
A Division of Thomas Nelson & Zondervan
1663 Liberty Drive
Bloomington, IN 47403
www.westbowpress.com
844.714.3454

ISBN: 978-1-6642-1773-7 (sc)
ISBN: 978-1-6642-1774-4 (e)

Library of Congress Control Number: 2020926025

Print information available on the last page.

WestBow Press rev. date: 01/15/2021

WESTBOW
PRESS®
A DIVISION OF THOMAS NELSON
& ZONDERVAN

Endorsements

For the past twenty-four years, I have been a pastor. Before that, I was a basketball coach. So most of my relationships have come by way of athletics or the local church. Such is the case with Brenda Keene. I met Brenda years ago when she was the equipment manager at East Tennessee State University, the university that produced my wife, Marsha, the school's leading scorer. God had our paths cross again last summer in North Carolina at Pine Needles for the Kay Yow Cancer Fund golf event. When Brenda shared the idea for this book with me, I knew immediately that it was hers to write. Brenda has the gift of encouragement and is so genuine when she communicates. She has a contagious love for Jesus Christ, and you can be sure that the pages that follow are born out of the overflow of her big heart touched by his amazing grace.

Andy Barnes, lead pastor of First Baptist Church, Gate City, Virginia

I have had the great privilege of knowing Brenda Keene for the last forty years and have seen firsthand her deep relationship with Christ. I am thrilled that her devotional on the fruits of the Spirit gives us an opportunity to catch a glimpse of that relationship.

May it serve to spur all of us on in our walk with the Lord.

Clyde Christensen, quarterbacks coach, Tampa Bay Buccaneers

I have known Brenda for over forty years and have witnessed her committed faith in Jesus Christ as well as her interest in photography. This picture book, which Brenda has created, is a way for her to share her passion for Christ and her enjoyment of photography. Through these pages and quotes, may you ponder the simpler, yet phenomenal qualities of God's creativity: his goodness in everyday living and his love for humankind.

O Lord what a variety you have made, and in wisdom you have made them all. The earth is full of your riches. (Psalm 104:24 The Living Bible)

Susan Yow, retired NCAA women's basketball coach

For more than thirty years, I have been blessed beyond measure through my friendship with Brenda Keene. Her love of life has been exhibited in ways that exemplify every fruit of the Spirit. It is only fitting that she brings to life words with pictures—words by which she lives her life and words that are shown in living color through her photography.

In a year when confusion, concern, and craziness seem to be in control, Brenda shows us that life is to be lived and we can find comfort in the everyday, simple blessings. Thank you, Bem, for these reminders and for showing us that his word serves as the lamp unto our feet and is the light unto our pathway!

Que Tucker, commissioner, North Carolina High School Athletic Association

We are honored that Brenda has chosen to use photographs of our farm and many of our horses as a backdrop to scripture. Her exceptional ability to capture nature's beauty through her outstanding photography combined with her faith and deep knowledge of the Lord's word has resulted in an inspiring book that can be enjoyed by all!

Robin Smith and Karen Freeman, Meadow Creek Farm

This book is dedicated in memory of those who LIVEaLIFE spreading love.

My dad, Gordon Joshua Keene, was killed at the age of twenty-nine in a coal mining accident in Bishop, West Virginia. He loved his family enough to work in an extremely dangerous job to provide for them. He had five children who were left to share his legacy of love, strength, and faithfulness.

My mom, Margaret M. (nee Click, Keene) Viars lived to be eighty-six. She lost her husband (my dad) when she was just twenty-eight and had five children to raise; she remarried, and had two more wonderful children. A courageous and strong woman whose life was proof of spreading the fruits of the Spirit.

My brother John L. Lewis Keene died at the age of twenty-nine. His legacy of love lives on through his son and grandchildren.

My brother-in-law Willard Wagner lived well and left a legacy of love through his wife, son, daughter, and grandson.

My great nephew Joshua Alan Cantrell was an adorable three-year-old when he went to be with the Lord. In his three short years, he had an amazing impact not only on his family but on hundreds if not thousands through his courageous fight with cancer. His legacy is carried on through Joshua Hoops for Hope and High Noon, which provides funds for scholarships to Floyd High School Seniors in Floyd, Virginia.

Our legacy is not the years we walk on earth but the lives that we touch during that time.

Contents

Preface

LIVEaLIFE spreading the fruits of the Spirit.

Proverbs 16:9 says in our hearts we plan our course, but God determines the steps. God is so faithful that he chooses steps that we would have never chosen because of the doubts we might have in our abilities. God has no doubts about the steps, for he knows our hearts and will provide the tools to accomplish his will. With the confidence to trust and depend upon the Holy Spirit and give all the glory to him, LIVEaLIFE spreading the fruits of the Spirit. As followers of Christ Jesus, we should follow the Spirit and spread these qualities.

In Galatians 5, he gives nine qualities that produce evidence that we are followers of Christ Jesus. These nine qualities are the fruits of the Spirit, which are love, joy, peace, patience, kindness, goodness, faithfulness, gentleness, and self-control. As we pray for the Holy Spirit to give us power and strength to live out these qualities each moment, we know there will be times we will fall short for we are all sinners and imperfect people asking for wisdom and guidance.

God's purpose, God's steps, and God's fruits of the Spirit.

Acknowledgments

This book exists because God has a perfect plan and purpose for all our lives, and this simple, ordinary page of this book is part of his purpose for my life. Thank you, Lord, for answering the prayers that left no doubt to proceed.

The Holy Spirit prompts us in many ways, and I have been blessed that he used family and friends who provided love with encouragement and time.

Thank you, and I love you all!

All photography is provided by the author. Locations of photos are the following:

- Meadow Creek Farm, Floyd, Virginia Insert image0.47
- Cowboy Angel Rockies
- Wagner Home, Virginia

Introduction

Fruits of the Spirit

Jesus said, "I will ask the Father, and he will give you another helper to be with you forever—the Spirit of Truth" (John 14:16–17 The Inspirational Study Bible: New Century Version).

Fruits of the Spirit are the qualities of the Holy Spirit working in our lives when we become believers and trust Christ as our Savior. These fruits portray the love of Christ.

What a difference our lives would make if daily we LIVEaLIFE spreading the fruits of the Spirit as we grow and mature in our faith in Christ Jesus.

God's message, God's purpose, and God's Spirit.

> Where can I go from your Spirit? Where can I flee from your presence? If I rise on the wings of the dawn, if I settle on the far side of the sea, even there your hand will guide me, your right hand will hold me fast. (Psalm 139:7-10 New International Version)

LIVEaLIFE soaring in grace.

LIVEaLIFE spreading Fruit of Love

Two of the greatest commandments in the Bible are to love God and love one another.

God is love! His word is our guidebook to loving him, others, and ourselves.

God's love is amazing and real; from the beginning, he has loved us. We were made in the image of God. He provided Adam and Eve with a life of paradise. Eve took her focus off God and allowed Satan to trick her into going against God's command not to eat of the Tree of Good and Evil. This is how sin entered the world.

The betrayal of Adam and Eve did not stop God from still loving humankind. God's love is so amazing that he provided a plan that would save us from our sins by sending his son, Christ Jesus, to die for all sins of humankind, the greatest sacrifice of love ever made. With that amazing gift of grace, we are free to choose a personal relationship with Christ Jesus and know our future is secure forever in his love.

As you read the word of God, you will find it is full of passages about his love for us from Genesis to Revelation. The passages are filled with guidance on how much he loves us, how we show him our love, and how to spread love to others. God's love is alive and has been available to humankind since the beginning words of love, encouragement, and inspiration. First John is just one book of God's words of great love for us and how much he wants us to love others.

> And love means living the way God commanded us to live. As you have heard from the beginning, his command is this, live a life of love. (2 John 1:6 NCV)

I'm thinking of this song that all the world knows: "Jesus loves me" and one of the lyrics is Jesus loves me, this I know For the Bible tells me so.

God's words, God purpose, and God's amazing love.

> God loved the world so much that he gave his one and only Son so that whoever believes in him may not be lost, but have eternal life. (John 3:16 NCV)

LIVEaLIFE to be transformed by God's grace.

LIVEaLIFE to love like Jesus.

LOVE

* is patient
* is kind
*does not envy
*does not boast
* is not proud
* is not rude or self-seeking
*keeps no record of wrongs
*rejoices with the truth
* always protects, trusts, hopes, and perseveres

Love never fails or ends (1 Corinthians 13:4–8 NIV).

LIVEaLIFE: Love in such a way to receive the prize.

Do you not know that in a race all the runners run, but only one gets the prize? Run in such a way to get the prize. (1 Corinthians 9:24 NIV)

LIVEaLIFE in the amazement of God's love.

God is love. Whoever lives in love lives in God, and God in him. In this way, love is made complete. (1 John 4:16–17 NIV)

LIVEaLIFE knowing the timeless love of God.

The Lord appeared to us in the past saying: "I have loved you with an everlasting love." (Jeremiah 31:3 NIV)

LIVEaLIFE in the wonder of God's work.

Great are the works of the Lord; they are pondered by all who delight in them. Glorious and majestic are his deeds, and his righteousness endures forever. (Psalm 111:2 NIV)

May the Lord make your love increase and overflow for each other and everyone else as ours does for you. (1 Thessalonians 3:12 NIV)

LIVEaLIFE overflowing with love.

LIVEaLIFE … reflecting God's heart.

As the water reflects the face, so a man's heart reflects the man. (Proverbs 27:19 NIV)

LIVEaLIFE spreading fruit of Joy

Let us not confuse joy with happiness. Joy is believing during life's most difficult moments. You *trust* Christ to meet your every need. It does not mean you will not experience sadness, grief, and other human emotions. You will. The fullness of joy is complete when we walk in the presence of Christ Jesus.

Happiness is based on your circumstances and people, and people disappoint and circumstances change. We will encounter trials. Happiness will be absent; joy will still be present for God has given us a spirit of hope for the future, no matter the circumstances of today, for he is the same forever.

Nehemiah 8:10 (NIV) says, "The JOY of the Lord is our strength."

It is when you hear God's word and understand that your life is for God's purpose.

God's words, God's purpose, and God's joy.

LIVEaLIFE so others will witness your joy.

"You are the light of the world," A city on a hill cannot be hidden. (Matthew 5:14–16 NIV)

LIVEaLIFE thriving in God's presence.

You have made known to me the path of life; you will fill me with Joy in your presence, with eternal pleasures at your right hand. (Psalm 16:11 NIV)

LIVEaLIFE running with the faith of salvation.

Though you have not seen him, you love him; even though you do not see him now, you believe in him and filled with in expressible glorious joy, for you are receiving the goal of your faith, the salvation of your souls. (1 Peter 1:8–9 NIV)

LIVEaLIFE bearing the fruit that lasts forever.

You did not choose me, but I chose you and appointed you to go and bear fruit—fruit that will last. (John 15:16 NIV)

This is the day the Lord has made; let us rejoice and be glad in it. (Psalm 118:24 NIV)

LIVEaLIFE rejoicing no matter the course.

LIVEaLIFE spreading fruit of Peace

Those who love your teachings will find true peace, and nothing will defeat them. (Psalm 119:165 NCV)

There are times that God's peace cannot be explained. It surpasses the world's knowledge of how it is even possible. Inner peace comes from when we remain in Christ and he remains in us.

There are times as a believer you might not even understand that overwhelming peace that we have. But it is deep within our souls. The empowering strength of the Holy Spirit is unexplainable.

God's words, God's purpose, and God's peace.

I leave you peace; my peace I give you. I do not give it to you as the world does. So, don't let your hearts be troubled or afraid. (John 14:27 NCV)

LIVEaLIFE with the Holy Spirit living within.

LIVEaLIFE with tranquility of hope.

May the God of Hope fill you with all joy and peace as you trust in him, so that you may overflow with hope by the power of the Holy Spirit. (Romans 15:13 NIV)

LIVEaLIFE never alone.

Yet I am not alone, for my Father is with me. "I have told you these things, so that in me you may have peace. In this world you will have trouble. But take heart! I have overcome the world." (John 16:32–33 NIV)

LIVEaLIFE: God is enough.

The lord is my shepherd I shall not be in want, He makes me lie down in green pastures, He leads me beside quiet waters, He restores my soul. (Psalm 23:1–3 NIV)

LIVEaLIFE spreading fruit of Patience

We have all heard the following: "Oh, to have the patience of Job." What an amazing and inspiring story of a man's life in the book of Job, for he lost all that he loved and owned yet persevered and endured such loss for he trusted in God's plan. His wife even encouraged him to give up and curse God, and his friends stated that he must have done something wrong for this to happen. Job stayed patient with his wife and friends, for God had given him all he had lost, and he would not forget that.

> When Job heard this, he got up and tore his robe and shaved his head to show how sad he was. Then he bowed down to the ground to worship God. He said "I was naked when I was born, and I will be naked when I die. The Lord gave these things to me, and he has taken them away. Praise the name of the Lord." In all this Job did not sin or blame God. (Job 1:20–22 NCV)

The passage is an extreme situation of a man who lost it all but still stayed patient because of his dedication to and love for God. We too can have that quality of endurance that Job had when we walk in the presence of Christ and know the power of the Holy Spirit working within us. We must remember that we live in a flawed world and all people and situations are not perfect. There will be moments when we must endure and persevere while trusting God. God allowed those moments, so take a breath and spread the quality of patience.

> God's plan, God's purpose, and God's patience.

LIVEaLIFE seeking God's wisdom.

You will seek me and find me when you seek me with all your HEART. (Jeremiah 29:13 NIV)

LIVEaLIFE with confidence in the promise.

You need to persevere so that when you have done the will of God, you will receive what he has promised. (Hebrews 10:36 NIV).

LIVEaLIFE secured in the will of God.

Even when you are old age and gray hairs

I am he, I am he who will sustain you and

I will carry you;

I will sustain you and I will rescue you. (Isaiah 46:4 NIV)

LIVEaLIFE eagerly waiting for the Lord.

For in this hope we were saved. But hope that is seen is no hope at all. Who hope for what he already has? But if we hope for what we do not yet have, we wait for it patiently. (Romans 8:24–25 NIV)

LIVEaLIFE spreading fruit of Kindness

The moment you extend kindness to others, you are making a statement that that person is worthy of your time. Simple kindness is so encouraging and empowering. You never know what that person needs, but God does.

God extends to us kindness through creation and others and his word of how worthy we are to him. That is all he wants us to do for others. God's kindness makes us feel special. Make someone else feel that way today.

> Do to others what you want them to do to you. This is the meaning of the law of Moses and the teaching of the prophets. (Matthew 7:12 NCV)

God's words, God purpose, and God's kindness.

LIVEaLIFE because God's kindness will never thirst again.

Jesus answered "Everyone who drinks this water will be thirsty again, but whoever drinks the water I give will never be thirsty. The water I give will become a spring of water gushing up inside that person giving eternal life." (John 4:13–14 NCV)

Christ accepted you, so you should accept each other, which will bring glory to God. (Romans 15:7 NCV)

LIVEaLIFE to extend your heart to others.

LIVEaLIFE to be richer.

Whoever gives to others will get richer; those who help others will themselves be helped. (Proverbs 11:25 NCV)

LIVEaLIFE with fragrance of kindness.

Don't ever forget kindness and truth. Wear them like a necklace. Write them on your heart as if on a tablet. Then you will be respected and will please both God and people. (Proverbs 3:3–4 NCV)

LIVEaLIFE spreading fruit of Goodness

David's prayer ends with him believing that goodness and mercy shall follow him all the days of his life. Goodness in this passage could be interpreted in many ways. For sure it is saying that when we dwell in the house of the Lord, he will protect and provide for us forever. So why would those of us who believe not ask to be filled with the fruit of goodness and spread that goodness?

Traits of the fruit of goodness are being gentle, loving, kind, and compassionate and giving and forgiving. These are characteristic and qualities of Christ Jesus.

Let us not just repeat the phrase "God is good." Let us spread the goodness of Christ Jesus to change hearts.

> Surely your goodness and love will be with me all my life,
> And I will live in the house of the Lord forever. (Psalm 23:6 NCV)

God's words, God's purpose, and God's goodness.

LIVEaLIFE
that
whatever is true,
whatever is noble,
whatever is right,
whatever is pure,
whatever is lovely,
whatever is admirable.

If anything is excellent or praiseworthy—think about such things. (Philippians 4:8 NIV)

However, I consider my life worth nothing to me, if only I may finish the race and complete the task the Lord Jesus has given me—task of testifying to the gospel of God's grace. (Acts 20:24 NIV)

LIVEaLIFE focused on God's grace.

LIVEaLIFE sharing God's love.

And do not forget to do good and to share with others, for with such sacrifices God is pleased. (Hebrews 13:16 NIV)

LIVEaLIFE in God's goodness.

I honestly believe I will live to see the Lord's goodness. (Psalm 27:13 NCV)

LIVEaLIFE spreading fruit of Faithfulness

Hebrews 11 is known as the faith chapter filled with individuals who are MVPs of faithfulness. These individuals never questioned God's faithfulness. And no matter the circumstances or what he might have asked them to do, they believed and fulfilled God's purpose. Some did not experience the promises of God on earth before they died but knew they would experience his everlasting promise. Eternal life is God's greatest promise of his faithfulness to every individual yesterday, today, and tomorrow. Christ Jesus is the author and perfector of our faith. Faithfulness should not be based on what God can do for us but on the fact that Christ Jesus died for us.

> Faith means being sure of the things we hope for and knowing that something is real even if we do not see it. (Hebrews 11:1 NCV)

God's words, God's grace, and God's faithfulness.

LIVEaLIFE to achieve God's purpose and prosper.

For I know the plans I have for you, declares the Lord, "plans to prosper you and not to harm you, plans to give you hope and a future." (Jeremiah 29:11 NIV)

Keep your roots deep in him and have your lives built on him. Be strong in the faith, just as you were taught, and always be thankful. (Colossians 2:7 NCV)

LIVEaLIFE strong in the faith.

But by Faith we eagerly await through the Spirit the righteousness for which we hope. (Galatians 5:5 NIV)

LIVEaLIFE with hope in Jesus.

Your love, O Lord, reaches to the heavens, your faithfulness to the skies. (Psalm 36:5 NIV)

LIVEaLIFE experiencing faithfulness that never ceases.

Let us hold firmly to the hope we have confessed, because we can trust God to do what he promised. (Hebrews 10:23 NCV)

LIVEaLIFE holding firmly on the promise of God.

LIVEaLIFE spreading fruit of gentleness.

Gentleness is a quality that tells us that we are to turn the other cheek. Spirit would have us to respond in such a way that we would be sincere and genuine and use soft-tone words to make our point.

> Which do you want: that I come to you with punishment or with love and gentleness? (1 Corinthians 4:21 NCV)

He wants us to reflect and asked that same question to us. Fruit of gentleness is a true quality that will help bring about unity. Our answer to the question with love and gentleness by God, and in return, we reflect the Spirit of Grace to others.

God's words, God's purpose, and God's gentleness.

LIVEaLIFE in the whisper of God's glory.

For the earth will be filled with the knowledge of the Glory of the Lord, as the waters cover the sea. (Habakkuk 2:14 NIV)

LIVEaLIFE soaking in the Gentleness

Let my teaching fall like rain and my words descend like dew, like showers on new grass, like abundant rain on tender plants. (Deuteronomy 32:2 NIV)

LIVEaLIFE speaking words that please the soul.

Pleasant words are a honeycomb, making people happy and healthy. (Proverbs 16:24 NCV)

LIVEaLIFE showing the strength of gentleness.

To speak no evil about anyone, to live in peace, and to be gentle and polite to all people. (Titus 3:2 NCV)

LIVEaLIFE spreading fruit of Self-control

Life is about self-control. Every day, we deal with temptations from the desires within. Satan knows our temptations and knows that as humans we are weak in our flesh. Fruit of self-control is from the Spirit of the Lord; this is how he resisted Satan himself and did not lose control and let Satan persuade him.

God provides us with that same power, the Holy Spirit, to shake Satan off and resist the temptation to lose control. We can do this by growing, remembering, and reflecting in our faith in Christ Jesus.

Jesus answered him, "It also says in the Scriptures, 'Do not test the Lord your God.'" (Matthew 4:7 NCV)

God's words, God's power, and God's self-control.

LIVEaLIFE with a spirit of power, love, and self-control.

God did not give us a spirit that makes us afraid but a spirit of power and love and self-control. (2 Timothy 1:7 NCV)

Because you have these blessings, do your best to add these things to your lives; to your Faith, add goodness; and to your goodness, add knowledge; and to your knowledge; add self-control, and to your self-control add patience; and to your patience, add service for God; and to your service for God, add kindness for your brothers and sisters in Christ; and to this kindness add love. If all these things are in you and are growing, they will help you to be useful and productive in your knowledge of our Lord Jesus Christ. (2 Peter 1:5–7)

LIVEaLIFE growing in the knowledge of our Lord Jesus Christ.

LIVEaLIFE knowing that God disciplines.

The Lord disciplines those he loves, and he punishes everyone he accepts as his child. (Hebrews 12:6 NCV)

LIVEaLIFE to be prepared in your faith.

Be self-controlled and alert. Your enemy the devil prowls around like a roaring lion looking for someone to devour. (1 Peter 5:8 NIV)

LIVEaLIFE knowing Jesus is the way.

Jesus answered, "I am the way, and the truth, and the life. The only way to the Father is through me." (John 14:6 NCV)

I hope you enjoyed the simple words and photos of my love for Christ Jesus. He gave me this task. It is one that I never dreamed would be a path he would lead me down.

The next photo is the answer that he provided. One Saturday morning during my devotions and prayer time, I asked him to give me a direct answer. He did by having this rock near a post on a trail on my walk. Even as I write these words, my heart is so full of the secure hope of his faithfulness. This I know because he lives in me.

God bless, and know God answers prayers.

God's plan, God's purpose, and God answers prayers.

LIVEaLIFE trusting in prayers and ready for the answer.

Trust the Lord with all your heart,
And don't depend on your own understanding,
Remember the Lord in all you do, and he will give you success. (Proverbs 3:5–6 NCV)

Printed in the United States
By Bookmasters